The Girl Who Wore Freedom

Christian Taylor

And

P.S. Wells

Special Edition

Normandy Project

Published by Normandy Project

www.normandystories.com

Dedication

To Dany,
The real girl who wore freedom.

And her family,
Jean-Marie, Flo, and Alyssia.

To the engaging people of Sainte Marie du Mont.

And to Hunter,
who introduced us to one another.

On the day I was born, France was free.
My mother named me Danielle
and clothed me in a soft, new dress she made.

My father held me up in the open window,
so I first heard the sounds of the neighbors
in our village of Sainte Marie du Mont.
I smelled the salt air of the nearby sea.

Soon, German soldiers arrived in my country.
Our cobble streets were filled
with the sharp clack-clack of their jack nail boots.
They guarded the beach
and used the church steeple as a watchtower.

We didn't have enough food.
My mother, Cecile, didn't have fabric
to sew clothes for our family.
My family and neighbors
were no longer free to move about.

My father, Paul, went far away to England
to fight for France's freedom.
While he was away, my mother traveled to the
nearby towns where she sold items to buy food for us.
A kind German soldier named Grandpa Paul,
cared for my older brother and me
while Mother was away.
Grandpa Paul knew the French people
had little food and no sugar.
For a treat, he gave me a small glass
with water and sugar.

My Papa returned home.
For four years, as I grew up,
my family waited to be free again.
The people of Sainte Marie du Mont
longed for liberty.

In the pre-dawn hours of June 6, 1944,
I woke to the noise of bee-like buzzing.
The boom of planes rolled in from the English Channel,
shaking the church steeple
and rattling Monsieur Blaziot's Butcher Shop window.
The fumes of airplane engines stung my nose.
I saw the sky filled with green and red
and white parachutes.

Mother's eyes were bright with excitement
as she hurried me into my worn clothes.
Gathered at the window,
my family watched gliders
sweep across the night
and gunfire spit from the church steeple.
"Is it possible?" Mother looked hopefully at Papa.
I held Mama's hand. "What is happening?"
"Les américains, les Anglais." My father
squeezed my shoulder. *"C'est le grand jour."*
"The Americans, the English," Mama repeated.
"They have come," said my brother, Francis,
"to deliver the big blow."

Papa stepped outside.
One by one, our neighbors came outdoors
until I thought all of Sainte Marie du Mont
had spilled from their homes into the night.
I clutched Mama's hand. "Is it dangerous to go out?"
Mama shook her head. "This is our right.
We remind them not to damage our town."
Too soon I felt sleepy. Tucked back into bed,
my mother's quilt drawn up to my chin,
I heard Mother go out to stand next to Papa.
I fell asleep to the tat-tat-tatting of guns
and the buzz of airplanes.

In the morning, I woke to the sound of ... Quiet.
No guns.
No airplanes.
No sharp clack-clack of boots.

As the sun rose, my parents, my brother, and I
peered out the window.
A man came from the beach
and calmly crossed the village square.

"They landed!" Papa lifted me so I could better see.
I squeezed his neck. "Who?"
"The Americans." My father went to greet
the newcomer who nodded his thanks.

The big American soldier went to the church.
He returned with the four German soldiers
who used the steeple as a watchtower.

"Last night," Mama said, "we went to sleep subjects of Germany and woke Americans." "We are free." Papa and Mama danced a circle with my brother and me.

American soldiers came from the beach.
Looking weary, the men went to the fountain
in our village square
and eagerly drank the cool, clear water.

More soldiers arrived on foot from Utah Beach.
They passed right by my house
that stood where the village and the beach met.

With my parents and brother,
I stood along the street to greet
the American soldiers who fought bravely.

I had never seen Americans.
Perhaps the Americans
had never seen French people.

The American soldiers smiled.
I waved back.
Passing by, the men reached into the packs
they carried and gave me
gum, chocolate, and candies.

The day my village was liberated
was the first time I tasted chocolate and candy.
Small and round with a hole in the center,
my favorite came in orange, lemon, and cherry.
They were Lifesavers and they were all delicious.

With my apron filled, I ran indoors,
dumped the treats onto the quilt on my bed,
and dashed back outside
to see the first tank rumble past our home
and through Sainte Marie du Mont.

In the following days,
some American soldiers continued past our village.
Others built a temporary port on Utah Beach
to provide supplies for the soldiers
fighting to liberate other towns.

The grateful French people
of Sainte Marie du Mont
invited the American soldiers
into our homes for meals.
We made them part of our families.

Three soldiers who often visited our family were "Tall Larry," "Big Smitty," and Harry Kropnicki. Harry's wife, Eleanor, was an American journalist who wrote about the new girl in her husband's life. Harry's new girl was five-year-old me.

"Danny" Patrix on her fourth birthday.

Eleanor Kropnicki was a bit concern-ed of late when she received letters from her husband in Normandy telling her there was another girl in his life. She wailed with an "I knew it would hap-pen!" until Harry sent a picture of the petite infant . . . Miss Danielle Patrix, age five. Needless to say, Mrs. K. is very much relieved.

The Americans shared canned pineapples.
They gave their torn parachutes to my mother.
Red parachutes had delivered weapons,
and white parachutes delivered the men.

Mother used the yards and yards of silk
to sew shirts and aprons.
From red and white parachutes,
she fashioned a dress for me
that looked like an American Flag.

In November of 1944, the port closed.
Our American friends left gifts
– a green Army jacket and the flag of freedom
that flew over Utah Beach.
Eventually the Americans returned to their own
homes and families in the United States.
But my family and I always remembered them
and the liberty they won for us.

In the spring of 1945,
the people of Sainte Marie du Mont
celebrated our freedom
with a D-Day ceremony on Utah Beach.
I wore my American flag dress made from parachutes.
In my new dress I was, "The Girl Who Wore Freedom."

Florence Boucherie

Epilogue

Dany wore her flag dress and participated in the annual D-Day commemoration ceremonies. When she outgrew the first flag dress, her mother sewed for her a new one.

Over the years, Dany celebrated Sainte Marie du Mont's liberation with famous men and war heroes including General Omar Bradley, General Lawton Collins, General Charles de Gaulle, General James Gavin, Colonel Robert Sink, John Steele, and General Maxwell Taylor.

On June 6, 2015, United States 506th Infantry Regiment 101st Airborne Division Specialist Hunter Taylor participated in Sainte Marie du Mont's D-Day celebration. Specialist Taylor and his family became friends with Dany Patrix and her family.

Dany's dress, made by her mother from red and white parachutes to look like an American flag, can be seen in the Utah Beach museum in Sainte Marie du Mont.

A plaque on Town Hall in the French town of Sainte Marie du Mont honors the bold and brave soldiers of the 101st American Airborne who risked everything to bring liberty.

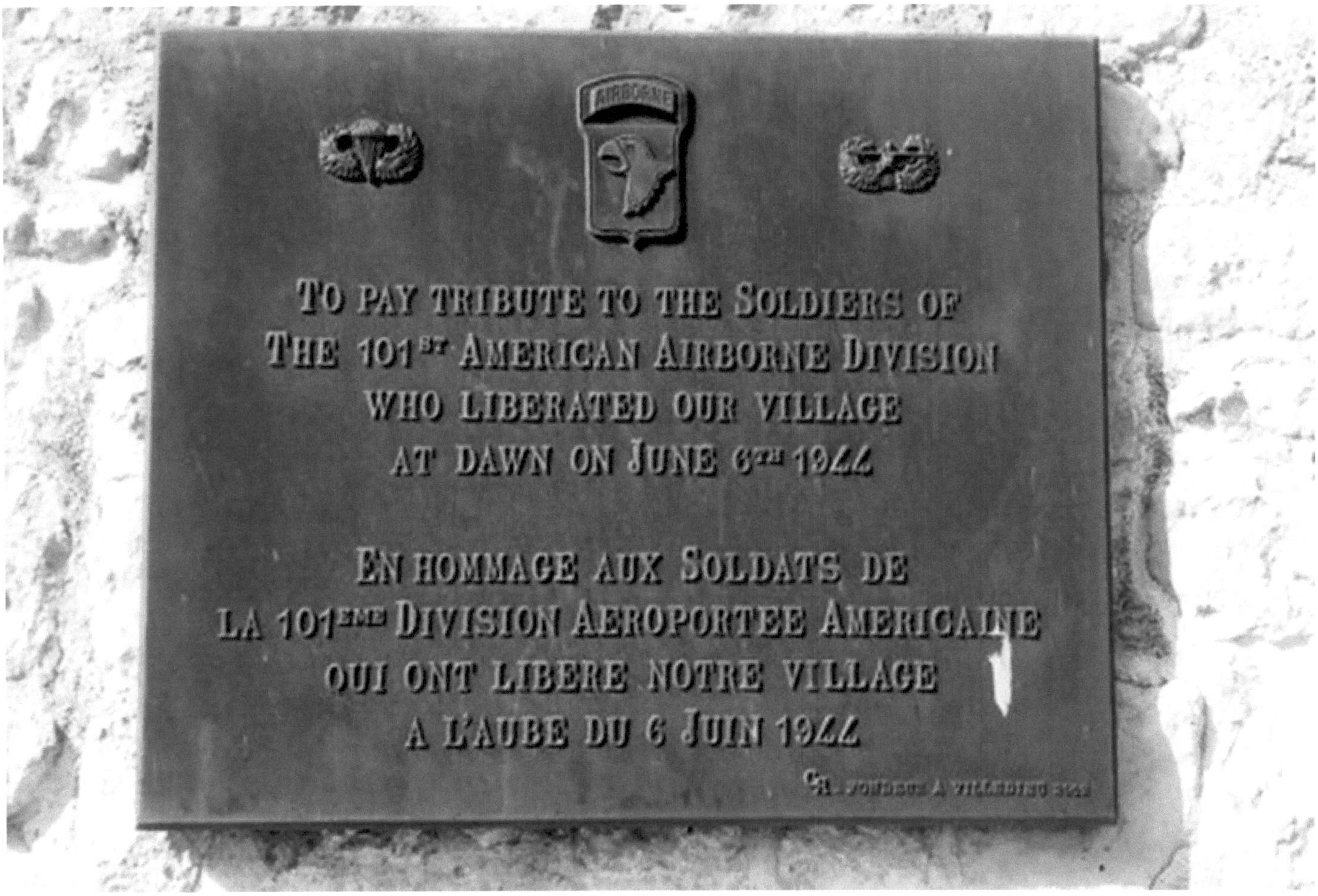
AIRBORNE
TO PAY TRIBUTE TO THE SOLDIERS OF
THE 101ST AMERICAN AIRBORNE DIVISION
WHO LIBERATED OUR VILLAGE
AT DAWN ON JUNE 6TH 1944
EN HOMMAGE AUX SOLDATS DE
LA 101EME DIVISION AEROPORTEE AMERICAINE
QUI ONT LIBERE NOTRE VILLAGE
A L'AUBE DU 6 JUIN 1944

Fun Facts About the Girl Who Wore Freedom

Paul Patrix (December 5, 1906 – 1970): Father to Dany, husband to Cecile, owner of Bar du 6 Juin

Cecile Patrix (May 26, 1912 – 1995): Mother to Dany, wife to Paul, ran a boarding house

Danielle "Dany" Patrix (May 26, 1939): The Girl Who Wore Freedom

Grandpa Paul: Older German soldier who did not want to fight for Hitler. A neighbor of the Patrix family, he babysat Dany and gave her sugar-water.

American Soldiers: Paratroopers and American soldiers shared chocolate, candy, and gum with Dany as they marched from Utah Beach and past her door. These brave men introduced Dany to pineapples in syrup, Lifesavers candy, and gave her a paratrooper jacket. The soldiers gave Cecile their silk parachutes so she could sew clothing for her family.

Larry Erolfin: "Tall Larry" was an American soldier and friend of the Patrix family. Because Dany often fell asleep in Larry's arms, he earned the nickname, Dany's Nanny.

Harry Kropnicki: An American soldier, Harry wrote to his wife that there was another girl in his life. He sent a photo of Dany to explain.

Timeline

March 16, 1935 – Germany's leader, Adolf Hitler, announced Germany had broken the Treaty of Versailles and built a large army intent on conquering other nations.

May 26, 1939 – Dany was born.

September 3, 1939 – In response to Germany's invasion of Poland, Britain and France declared war on Germany.

June 18, 1940 – General Charles de Gaulle called the French to resist German invasion. Dany's father, Paul, traveled to England to join the Free French Movement, leaving Cecile, Francis, and Dany in Sainte Marie du Mont.

June 22, 1940 – France surrendered to Germany. German soldiers moved into Sainte Marie du Mont, set up headquarters in the church, and lived in flats around the village square and a few doors from Dany.

1941 – Dany's father, Paul, returned home.

June 6, 1944 – D-Day. Allied forces, including American soldiers, came to Normandy to liberate France from German occupation.

June 7, 1944 – Sustainment operations, including the establishment of an American base on Utah Beach, began in Sainte Marie du Mont.

November 4, 1944 – The Port at Utah Beach closed.

May 9, 1945 – Victory in Europe Day. The Allied Forces formally accept Nazi Germany's unconditional surrender.

September 2, 1945 – Imperial Japan formally surrenders. World War II ends.

June 6, 1945 – The first Commemoration Ceremony is held, celebrating the liberation of Sainte Marie du Mont and France.

June 6, 2015 – During the D-Day celebration, Dany met another soldier from the United States 506th Infantry Regiment 101st Airborne Division. Specialist Hunter Taylor and his family became friends with Dany and her family.

About the Authors

Christian Taylor

Christian Taylor's 35-year entertainment industry career spans stage, screen, and sound booth. Talent, producer, director, casting director, writer, and coach, Christian serves as co-host of the *Holy Post* with Phil Vischer and Skye Jethani. Christian began her career interviewing Senators on Capitol Hill with the TV/Radio department of the Senate, *The Senate Republican Conference.*

P.S. Wells

History buff, and tropical island votary, PeggySue Wells parasails, skydives, snorkels, scuba dives, and has taken (but not passed) pilot training. Writing from the 100-Acre wood in Indiana, Wells is the bestselling author of twenty-nine books including
The Slave Across the Street,
Bonding With Your Child Through Boundaries,
Slavery in the Land of the Free,
Homeless for the Holidays,
and *Chasing Sunrise.*

CPSIA information can be obtained
at www.ICGtesting.com
Printed in the USA
LVHW072116111222
734987LV00013B/692

* 9 7 8 0 5 7 8 4 8 5 2 6 3 *